P9-CCX-847

This Is a Let's-Read-and-Find-Out Science Book®

GRAVITY IS A MYSTERY

REVISED EDITION

By Franklyn M. Branley   Illustrated by Don Madden

THOMAS Y. CROWELL NEW YORK

Other Recent Let's-Read-and-Find-Out Science Books® You Will Enjoy

The *Let's-Read-and-Find-Out Science Book* series was originated by Dr. Franklyn M. Branley, Astronomer Emeritus and former Chairman of The American Museum–Hayden Planetarium, and was formerly co-edited by him and Dr. Roma Gans, Professor Emeritus of Childhood Education, Teachers College, Columbia University. For a complete catalog of Let's-Read-and-Find-Out Science Books, write to Thomas Y. Crowell Junior Books, Harper & Row, Publishers, Inc., 10 East 53rd Street, New York, NY 10022.

Gravity Is a Mystery
Text copyright © 1986 by Franklyn M. Branley
Illustrations copyright © 1986 by Don Madden
All rights reserved. No part of this book may be
used or reproduced in any manner whatsoever without
written permission except in the case of brief quotations
embodied in critical articles and reviews. Printed in
the United States of America. For information address
Thomas Y. Crowell Junior Books, 10 East 53rd Street,
New York, N.Y. 10022. Published simultaneously in
Canada by Fitzhenry & Whiteside Limited, Toronto.
Designed by Trish Parcell
10 9 8 7 6 5 4 3 2 1
Revised Edition

Library of Congress Cataloging-in-Publication Data
Branley, Franklyn Mansfield, 1915–
  Gravity is a mystery.

  (Let's-read-and-find-out science book)
  Summary: Explains in simple text and illustrations
what is known about the force of gravity.
  1. Gravitation—Juvenile literature. 2. Gravity—
Juvenile literature. [1. Gravity] I. Madden,
Don, 1927–   ill. II. Title. III. Series.
QC178.B66 1986   531'.14   85-48247
ISBN 0-690-04526-3
ISBN 0-690-04527-1 (lib. bdg.)

  (A Harper Trophy book)
  (Let's-Read-and-Find-Out book)
ISBN 0-06-445057-0

Suppose you could dig a hole to the center of the earth. Suppose you dug right past the center. If you dug long enough and deep enough, you would come out in the Indian Ocean.

If you jumped into the hole, you would fall down. Down and down you would go.

You would fall faster and faster toward the center of the earth. When you reached the center, you would be going so fast you could not stop. You would go right past the center.

Then, on the other side, you would move up and away from the center of the earth. You would fall *up* for a while. You would go slower and slower. Then you would stop. You would almost get to the Indian Ocean—but not quite.

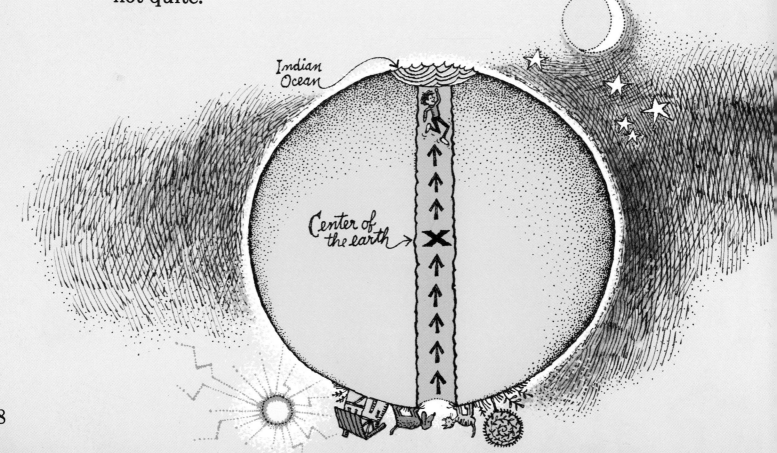

Now you would fall back toward the center of the earth. You would go faster and faster, right past the center. But you would not quite reach your starting point.

Back and forth you would go. Each time you would go a shorter distance past the center.

Back and forth, back and forth.

Gravity would make you fall toward the center of the earth. When you moved past the center, gravity would pull you back again.

After a long, long time you would stop moving. You would stay at the center of the earth.

Gravity pulls everything toward the center of the earth.

When you run downhill,
gravity pulls you.

When you throw a ball up,
gravity pulls it down.

When you sit, gravity holds you down.

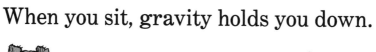

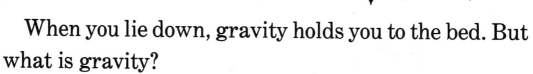

When you lie down, gravity holds you to the bed. But
what is gravity?

We know gravity is everywhere, even though we can't see it. We know it pulls on every rock, every grain of sand. It pulls on everything. But no one knows exactly what gravity is. That's why we say gravity is a mystery.

The gravity of the earth pulls everything toward the center of the earth. You know this when you try to lift a heavy stone. Gravity pulls it down. The more the stone weighs, the more gravity pulls on it. To lift the stone, you must pull up harder than gravity pulls down.

Lift your little brother; then try to lift your father.
The more they weigh, the harder it is to lift them.

16

You already know how much gravity pulls on you. Do you weigh 60 pounds? That means the pull of the earth's gravity on you is 60 pounds. How much you weigh tells how much gravity pulls on you. How much a stone weighs tells how much gravity pulls on the stone.

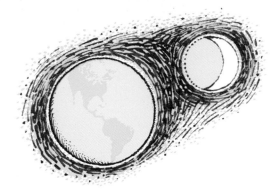

The earth has gravity, and so does the moon. The earth's gravity pulls you toward the center of the earth. If you were on the moon, the moon's gravity would pull you toward the center of the moon. The moon has less gravity than the earth has. This means the moon's gravity does not pull as hard as the earth's gravity.

Do you weigh 60 pounds? If you were on the moon, you would weigh only 10 pounds. The pull of the moon's gravity on you would be only 10 pounds.

Weight on Earth: 60 lbs.

Weight on the moon: 10 lbs.

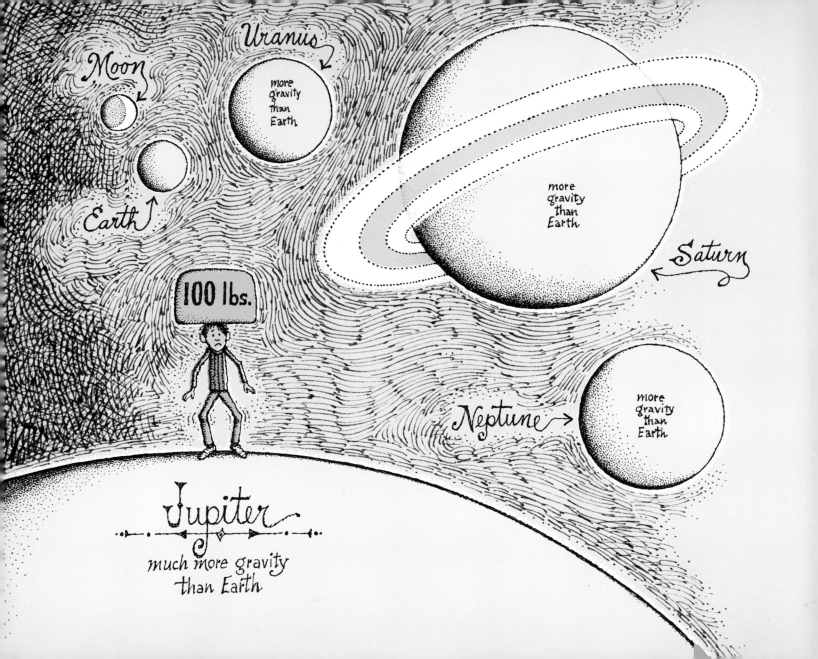

Sun

The earth and the moon have gravity, and so does each of the nine planets. Jupiter, Saturn, Uranus, and Neptune have more gravity than the earth has. On any of these planets you would weigh more than you weigh on the earth. On Saturn, Uranus, and Neptune you would weigh only a little more. On Jupiter you would weigh a lot more.

Do you weigh 60 pounds? On Jupiter you would weigh about 160 pounds.

Gravity on Mercury, Venus, Mars, and Pluto is less than it is on Earth. On these planets you would weigh less than you weigh on the earth. On Venus you would weigh only a little less. But on Mercury, Mars, and Pluto you would weigh a lot less.

Do you weigh 60 pounds? On Mercury and Mars you would weigh only about 20 pounds. Even less on Pluto.

Suppose you weigh 60 pounds. This is about how much you would weigh on the moon, on each of the planets, and on the sun:

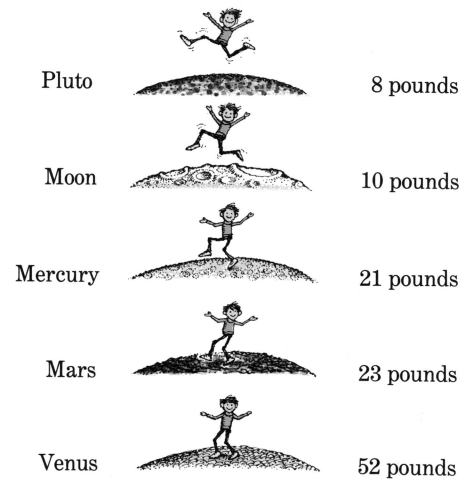

Pluto	8 pounds
Moon	10 pounds
Mercury	21 pounds
Mars	23 pounds
Venus	52 pounds

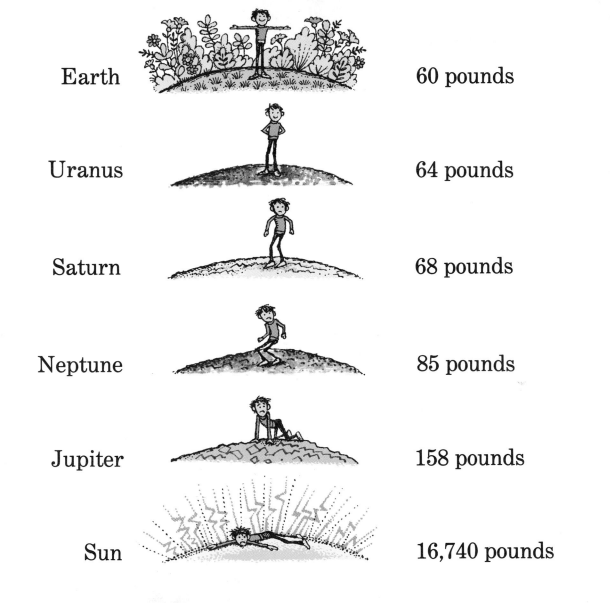

Earth — 60 pounds

Uranus — 64 pounds

Saturn — 68 pounds

Neptune — 85 pounds

Jupiter — 158 pounds

Sun — 16,740 pounds

25

If you were on Mars, gravity would pull you toward the center of Mars. You could stand up and sit down just as you can on the earth. It would be easier to move around, though, because you would weigh less. You could run in big giant steps because gravity on Mars is much less than it is on the earth.

You would weigh a lot more on Jupiter than you do on the earth. It would be harder to move around on that planet. Your legs would get tired from carrying you. Try running with a hundred-pound pack on your back. That's what it would be like all the time on Jupiter.

Gravity is everywhere—on the earth, on the moon, on Jupiter, Mars, and all the other planets. The sun has gravity too, and so does every other star.

The gravity of the earth holds things on the earth. It holds down rugs and tables, and you and me.

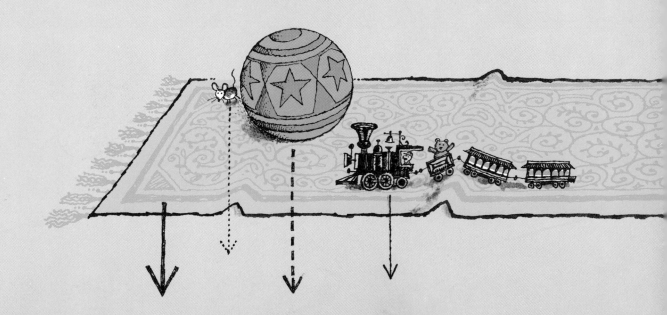

29

Gravity makes a ball come down. It makes us work
hard to lift a heavy stone.

We know where gravity is: it is everywhere. And we know what gravity does.

But no one knows exactly what gravity is.

Gravity is a mystery.